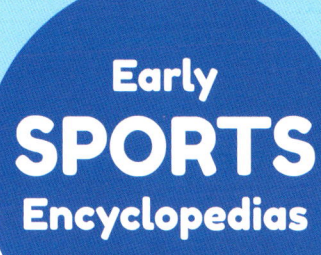

Early SPORTS Encyclopedias

DANCE

by Heather L. Bode

Early Encyclopedias

An Imprint of Abdo Reference
abdobooks.com

abdobooks.com

Published by Abdo Reference, a division of ABDO, PO Box 398166, Minneapolis, Minnesota 55439. Copyright © 2024 by Abdo Consulting Group, Inc. International copyrights reserved in all countries. No part of this book may be reproduced in any form without written permission from the publisher. Early Encyclopedias™ is a trademark and logo of Abdo Reference.

Printed in China

052023
092023

Editor: Priscilla An
Series Designers: Candice Keimig, Joshua Olson

Library of Congress Control Number: 2022949124

Publisher's Cataloging-in-Publication Data

Names: Bode, Heather L., author.
Title: Dance / by Heather L. Bode
Description: Minneapolis, Minnesota: Abdo Reference, 2024 | Series: Early sports encyclopedias | Includes online resources and index.
Identifiers: ISBN 9781098291273 (lib. bdg.) | ISBN 9781098277451 (ebook)
Subjects: LCSH: Dance--Juvenile literature. | Dance teams--Juvenile literature. | Team sports--Juvenile literature. | Sports--History--Juvenile literature. | Encyclopedias and dictionaries--Juvenile literature.
Classification: DDC 796.03--dc23

CONTENTS

Introduction **4**
    Basics of Dance 8
    Basics of Ballet 18
    Basics of Ballroom 26
    Basics of Hip-Hop 42
    Basics of Jazz 54
    Basics of Tap 62
    All about Ballet 70
    All about Ballroom 82
    All about Hip-Hop 94
    All about Jazz 104
    All about Tap 114
    All about Dancing for Life 122

Glossary **126**
To Learn More **127**
Index **127**
Photo Credits **128**

INTRODUCTION

Dancing with family can be a fun activity.

What Is Dance?

Dance is all about movement. People usually dance to the rhythm of music. They can dance to show how they feel.

There are many types of dances all over the world. Dance can be used to tell a story. It is a form of art. Dance can also share different cultures and traditions. It can even be used when practicing religious beliefs. But many people dance for fun. They dance with friends, family, and even strangers.

Some people dance professionally. They train for many years to make their bodies more flexible. They learn from experienced dancers. They perform in front of large crowds.

Working together is important when dancing with a group.

INTRODUCTION

History of Dance

No one knows who the first dancers were. No one knows why people began to dance. But people have been dancing for a long time. Ancient cave paintings in India show people dancing. Ancient peoples in Greece and Egypt danced. They did this to mark life events. People danced when someone gave birth. They danced at weddings and at funerals. People also

Cave paintings show that dancing is a very old form of expression.

Traditional dances can be an important part of religions or cultures.

danced to worship their gods. Ancient Greeks choreographed dances too. These dances were done in theaters. As people spread around the world, dance went with them.

BASICS OF DANCE

Dancers train their muscles so they can move their bodies into different shapes.

Almost anyone can dance. People might study different kinds of dance. They can pick their favorites. Dancing is a way to be creative. It helps people's muscles grow strong. Dancing

FUN FACT!

So You Think You Can Dance and *Dancing with the Stars* are popular dance TV shows. These shows introduce people to many forms of dance.

helps people control their bodies. It can improve a person's balance. A dancer may become more flexible. Dancing also keeps the brain active.

Dancing can help get rid of stress.

BASICS OF DANCE

Foot Basics

Dancers use different parts of their feet. The ball of the foot connects the toes to the foot. When people stand on their tiptoes, they use the balls

Dancers learn different types of footwork.

ball of the foot

of their feet. The heel is the back of the foot. The arch is the part between the ball and the heel. It helps give the foot shape. Dance teachers may say, "Put weight on the balls of your feet," or "Lean back on your heels." This helps dancers know what part of the foot to use.

heel

arch

BASICS OF DANCE

Mirrors help people see their dance teacher's movements and instructions.

Dance Studios

Most dancers go to dance studios to practice. A studio usually has a large open floor. The floor may be wooden. A large mirror is usually on one wall. This allows the dancers to watch their movements. Ballet barres are usually on the other walls. These are handrails. They help dancers balance. Studios also have a sound system for music.

Ballet barres help dancers balance.

BASICS OF DANCE

Private lessons allow teachers to pay more attention to a dancer's strengths and weaknesses.

Some studios teach one type of dance. Others teach many kinds of dance styles, like ballet, hip-hop, and jazz. People interested in learning dance should visit nearby studios. Some studios let people try out a class. This helps them decide if they want to sign up. It is important for people to find a studio where they feel comfortable.

Most dance classes are group classes. Group classes are good for beginners. Students can meet other dancers. They can learn by watching other dancers. Some people take private lessons. These are one-on-one lessons with a teacher. The teacher can help the student improve faster. Private lessons can also help if the student gets nervous dancing around a group of people.

The Dance Bag

Dancers carry a dance bag to class. Bags can hold shoes and extra clothes. Many dancers keep a snack and a water bottle in their bags. Bandages and hair accessories are useful too. These items help dancers be prepared for class.

BASICS OF DANCE

Dance Safety

People may get hurt when they dance. Common injuries can be from a dancer's shoes. Blisters may form. This happens if a dancer's shoes do not fit properly. It can also happen when a dancer is wearing new shoes.

Dancers may fall. They can make a wrong step and twist an ankle. They may even break a bone. But there are many ways to stay safe while dancing. Dancers do warm-up stretches. This gets their muscles ready to work. Dancers should not try new and difficult moves without a teacher. Dance teachers know their students. They decide when students

Stretching and using the right shoes can keep dancers from getting injured.

It is important to take breaks and drink water while practicing.

are ready for new steps. They can help dancers use proper techniques.

There are also things dancers can do when class is over. Heart-healthy activities help dancers. They can swim or bike. They can run or walk. Food and water are important fuel for dancers. People also need to get plenty of rest. Rest helps the body heal and grow. All these things help a dancer's body stay strong.

BASICS OF BALLET

Formal ballet training typically starts at a young age.

Ballet is a popular classical dance. A person can begin ballet at a young age. Dancers learn basic arm and feet positions.

Female ballet dancers wear tights and leotards. Male dancers wear tights or shorts with a T-shirt. Snug clothing makes it easier for dancers to jump and twirl. Teachers can also see the dancer's posture better. Students with long hair wear it up in a bun. This keeps hair out of their eyes. Some dancers wear skirts or shorts over their leotards.

All ballet dancers begin in full-soled ballet shoes. These shoes are soft. They are usually made of leather or fabric. Full-soled shoes help dancers learn how to point their toes. This helps build muscle in the feet. Later, dancers can wear split sole shoes. These shoes are more flexible.

Beginner ballet dancers wear full-soled shoes, *left*. Advanced dancers can wear split soles, *right*.

BASICS OF BALLET

New ballet shoes do not have a right or left shoe. The shoes form to the dancer's feet. Ballet shoes have an elastic drawstring. This helps the shoes fit the dancer's feet. Elastic straps help hold the shoe in place.

Dancers must take good care of their shoes. Some fabric ballet shoes can be washed. Leather ballet shoes can only be spot cleaned. Dancers should not wear their ballet shoes outside. Rocks, rain, and snow can damage shoes.

FUN FACT!
The first ballet shoes did not look like today's shoes. They had heels.

Pointe Shoes
Pointe shoes are fabric shoes. The tips of the shoes have a toe box made of cardboard hardened by glue. Only advanced dancers wear pointe shoes. This is because people's bones are not fully formed until they are 13 to 15 years old. Starting pointe too early can lead to foot injuries. Dance teachers decide when students are ready for pointe.

Reverence is often done at the end of a performance.

Many ballet classes begin at the barre. This is where dancers warm up. The barre also helps dancers find their center of balance. Barre exercises prepare dancers for centre. Centre takes place in the middle of the studio. Dancers work on jumps and spins. Ballet classes usually end with reverence. Dancers bow or curtsy to their teacher. They do this to say thank you. It is part of ballet tradition.

BASICS OF BALLET

Five Positions

Ballet has five basic positions. Each position is connected. A dancer's feet and hips are turned out in all five positions. Turnout is when dancers rotate their hips. The inside of their feet and legs faces forward.

First position keeps the legs straight. The dancer's heels touch. The toes point outward. Second position is similar. But a dancer's feet are spread shoulder-width apart. Third position is not common for advanced dancers. In this

first position

second position

position, the heel of one foot lines up with the center of the other foot.

In fourth position, one foot is in front of the other. There is space between the feet. The heel of the front foot lines up with the toes of the back foot. In fifth position, there is no space between the feet. The toes of the back foot touch the heel of the front foot.

> The five positions are important for ballet dancers. This is because all ballet moves begin or end in one of the five positions.

third position

fourth position

fifth position

BASICS OF BALLET

Key Movements

Ballet steps have French names. This is because the first ballet school was in France. It is known as the Paris Opera Ballet.

The plié is a key ballet movement. This is when a dancer keeps his feet flat on the floor. Then he bends his knees. A relevé is when a dancer straightens his knees. He lifts his heels off the floor. He balances on the balls of his feet. Another important ballet

A tendu is when a dancer extends one leg while pointing the toe.

An arabesque can be done on a flat foot or on the toes.

move is the passé. For this movement, a dancer stands on one leg. The other leg bends at the knee. The toes of the bent leg touch the straight leg above the knee.

An arabesque is a pose. This is when a dancer balances on one leg. The other leg is stretched out in the air behind the dancer. A pirouette is a spin. When doing this move, dancers lift one leg into passé. Then they turn all the way around.

Contemporary Dance

Contemporary dance is different from ballet. Dancers are usually barefoot. They focus on showing emotion. Dancers also do a lot more floor work than leg work.

BASICS OF BALLROOM

Ballroom dance includes many kinds of dances. Each ballroom dance has special steps. It has special rhythms. But ballroom dances have some things in common. They are all partner dances. They are danced in closed hold position. This means that the partners' bodies touch at certain points.

There are different types of holds in ballroom dancing.

It is important for partners to move together with the music.

BASICS OF BALLROOM

Understanding the roles of a lead and follow are essential in ballroom dance.

Lead and Follow

Each dance partnership has a lead and a follow. Some competitions say men have to be leads. Women are follows. Others allow same-gender partnerships. In these partnerships, dancers can choose whether to learn lead or follow.

The lead chooses what steps to do. He or she can signal the follow by making a hand signal. The follow responds to the lead. Both partners work together. They move smoothly. Partners do not talk while dancing. Instead, they communicate with body movements. This takes a lot of time and practice.

Partners need to practice together.

BASICS OF BALLROOM

Frame is important in ballroom. This is how dancers position their bodies. It includes how they hold their arms, stand, and touch their dancing partner. In most ballroom dances, the rules of frame are the same. Partners face each other. The lead's left hand holds the follow's

Knowing the four points of where the arms and hands connect is important to hold frame correctly.

Stretching can help a dancer have good posture.

right hand. The lead's right hand goes on the follow's back. The follow's left hand goes on the lead's shoulder, arm, or back.

Holding frame is important. Dancers must have good posture. A dancer's head should be held high. Holding frame helps partners move together. Sometimes dancers break frame. They dance on their own and go back to their partners.

BASICS OF BALLROOM

Dancers can practice their steps without a partner.

Ballroom Steps

Every ballroom dance has a basic step pattern. The pattern is different for each dance. People learn the dance's basic step first. The basic step is the most important. After dancers have mastered the basics, they can try other moves.

Some ballroom dances are choreographed to music. Social dances and competitions are not. Dancers do not know what song will play. The lead chooses and directs the steps. That way, their partner can follow them smoothly.

The cha-cha is a Latin and rhythm dance. Cha-cha dancers mainly move their hips and legs. The upper body is kept still.

Most cha-cha dances start with the rock step. First, the leaders take one step back with their right foot. Then they shift their weight to the right hip. They tap their left foot. Afterward, they do a triple step.

The cha-cha has a lot of quick steps.

BASICS OF BALLROOM

People can learn ballroom dancing starting as young as five years old.

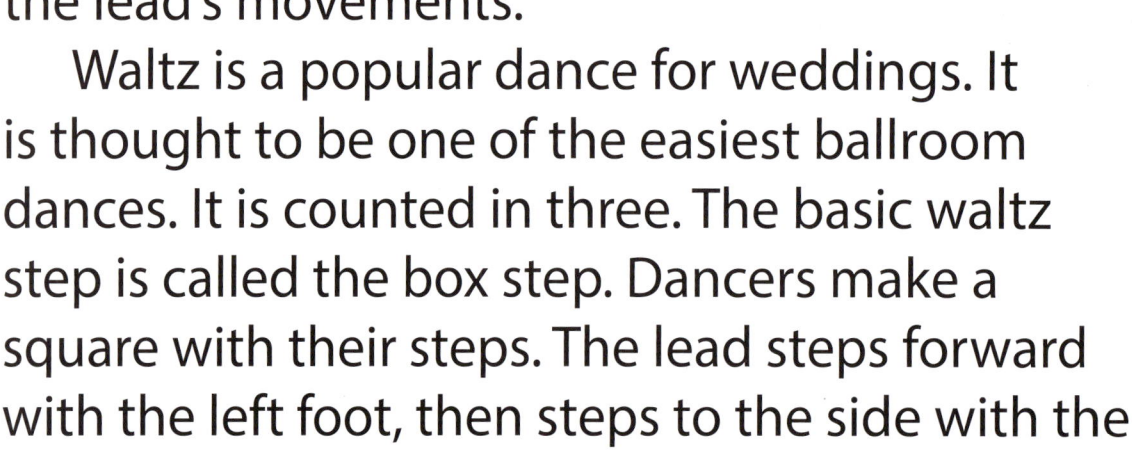

This is when leaders take their right foot and place it next to the left. Then they step on their right foot, then their left foot. Then the pattern starts over again. Follows face the lead. They do the same pattern. But they mirror the lead's movements.

Waltz is a popular dance for weddings. It is thought to be one of the easiest ballroom dances. It is counted in three. The basic waltz step is called the box step. Dancers make a square with their steps. The lead steps forward with the left foot, then steps to the side with the right foot. The left foot follows the right foot. Then the lead steps back with the right foot. The lead steps to the side with the left foot. Then the feet come together. Follows do the same pattern. But they start with the right foot going back.

Advanced dancers rotate as they do the box step. They bend and straighten their knees. This makes them rise and fall like waves.

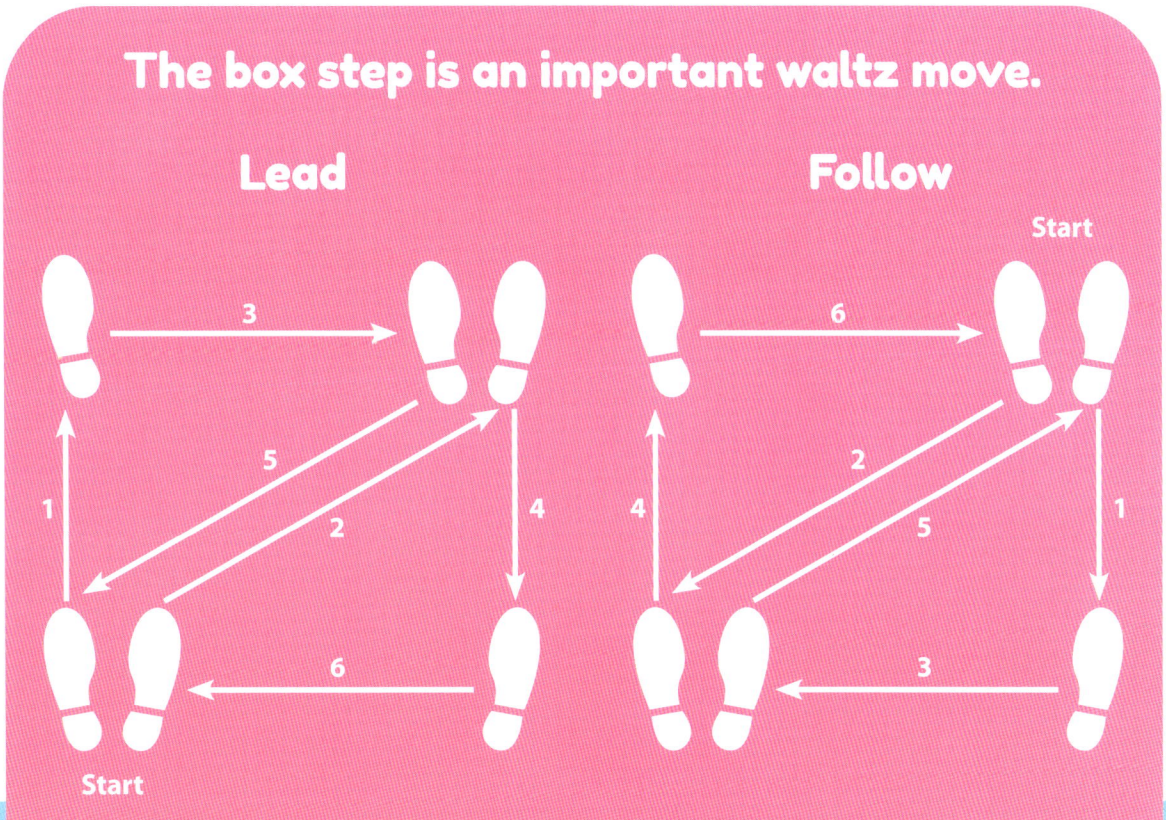

The box step is an important waltz move.

BASICS OF BALLROOM

Ballroom Attire

Ballroom shoes have suede soles. This lets dancers slide and turn. The suede soles can get matted down. This makes the shoes slippery. Dancers can brush the soles of their shoes with a brush that has metal bristles. Brushing the soles helps the shoes last longer. It also keeps the shoes from slipping. Ballroom shoes should only be worn inside.

Older ballroom dancers often wear fishnet tights.

Closed-toed shoes protect a dancer's toes.

Ballroom dancers wear heeled shoes. Shoes for young girls have low, wide heels. Older dancers wear high heels. Sometimes female dancers wear shoes with low heels for practice. Men's ballroom shoes have heels too.

A dancer may wear different shoes depending on the dance style. Men's standard or smooth shoes have a shorter heel than Latin shoes. Women often wear open-toed shoes for Latin.

BASICS OF BALLROOM

Closed-toed shoes are more common for smooth or standard ballroom dances. There are also shoes that work for both styles. Dancers should always wear shoes that support their feet. It is important to get the right fit.

Ballroom outfits for practicing are simple. Dancers wear clothes they can move in easily. They do not want to get too hot. Some dancers

During practice, dancers might wear more casual and comfortable clothing.

might wear dress pants or a skirt. Others wear comfortable workout clothes.

Young dancers have strict rules for competition clothing. Competitions can have different rules. Boys usually wear black pants. They wear white shirts with long sleeves. Boys can wear bow ties or straight ties. They may wear black shoes and socks. Girls can wear dresses.

Young ballroom dancers usually cannot wear shiny fabrics in competition.

BASICS OF BALLROOM

Dancers need to wear the right type of clothing during competitions.

They can also wear a leotard or shirt with a skirt or pants. Skirts are typically knee length. Dresses have to be simple and one solid color. Clothes cannot have jewels or other decorations. Girls can wear tights or white socks with their dance shoes. Young dancers are not allowed to wear makeup.

Adult ballroom dancers usually wear fancier costumes. Women can wear dresses, skirts, or pants. Dresses for Latin dancing are shorter. Standard or smooth dresses are long. Sleeves can be any length. Some dancers wear gloves or floats. A float is a piece of fabric attached to the dress. Men wear black pants. They can wear colorful shirts for Latin dances. They might wear a vest. Men usually wear suits for smooth and standard. They wear white shirts. Adults usually can have decorations on their costumes.

Dresses for Latin dancing often have fringe or ruffles at the bottom.

BASICS OF HIP-HOP

Hip-hop has many styles. Break dancing, popping, and locking are hip-hop dances. Hip-hop dances can be performed alone or with a group.

Dancers can wear normal sneakers. They might wear baggy pants and sweatshirts. Loose clothing helps dancers move quickly. Hip-hop dancers sometimes wear hats.

Hip-hop is not just a dance style but a cultural movement.

Adidas Superstars

Nike Air Force 1

Iconic Sneakers in Hip-Hop

Sneakers are an important part of hip-hop culture. These shoes were made popular by well-known Black hip-hop artists and icons.

Air Jordan

Puma Suede

BASICS OF HIP-HOP

Break Dancing

Break dancing is also called breaking. Dancers are called breakers, b-boys, or b-girls. Breakers use different types of moves. These are toprock, drops, downrock, power moves, and freezes.

Toprock moves are done in a standing position. These are simple moves that help the breaker warm up. The two-step is a toprock move. Breakers stand with their feet together. They take a step to the right. They bring the left foot over. It touches the floor by

Breakers can add their own freestyle.

Breakers drop to the beat of the music.

the right foot. Then the left foot steps to the left. The right foot meets the left. This step-touch move is common in other dance styles too.

Drops move the breaker to the floor. During a knee drop, a breaker stands on one leg. The opposite leg bends at the knee. The foot of the bent leg hooks behind the straight knee. The straight leg bends. The knee drops to the floor. Breakers use their hands to balance. The toes of the bent leg help protect the knee.

BASICS OF HIP-HOP

Breakers focus on their body positions when practicing windmills.

Downrock moves are floor movements. The dancer's hands and feet support the body. The six-step is a downrock move. The dancer starts in a crouch. The dancer's feet and hands are on the floor. Dancers cross their legs and arms in a circular pattern.

Power moves are acrobatic moves. They include spins. Breakers spin on their backs.

How a breaker freezes in a performance is important.

Cyphers help dancers learn from each other.

Some spin on their heads. The windmill is a power move. This is when a breaker's legs make a V in the air. His weight is on his shoulders or hands. His legs spin around like a windmill.

Breakers usually freeze at the end of a dance. They hold or freeze their bodies in the air. People might need upper body strength to do these moves.

Cyphers are informal dances. Breakers take turns dancing in the middle of a circle. One breaker is surrounded by other break dancers. Waiting dancers cheer and watch. Breakers try to show their best moves.

BASICS OF HIP-HOP

Popping and Locking

Popping is a style of dance where people flex their muscles to the beat. Parts of the body snap into new shapes. These look like jerky movements. But they are always in time to the music.

Poppers use isolation. This is when one part of the body moves. The rest of the body stays still. Poppers mix body motion isolations with freezes. A move called the robot uses isolations. It also uses dime stops. This is when dancers stop suddenly in the middle of their dance.

Waving is a dance move in popping.

Locking started out as a solo dance.

In locking, dancers listen to the rhythm of the music. In the middle of quick movements, they stop, or lock, in a certain position. They freeze in rhythm with the music. After holding the position, they go back to their original speed.

The muscleman is a common pose. Lockers hold their arms out to their sides. They curl their arms up. They lock in place. This is also called an uplock.

BASICS OF HIP-HOP

The robot dance move tries to mimic a dancing robot or mannequin.

Basic Hip-Hop Moves

Breakers, poppers, and lockers blend moves. They create their own unique styles. Some moves are seen in other kinds of dances.

Hip-hop dancers practice the robot. They start by picking one body part, like their arms or legs. They practice moving it back and forth. Then they freeze. Dancers can even wobble after each move to try and act like a robot.

Sliding and gliding are similar to each other. People doing these moves look like they are walking in place. Sliding starts with a forward movement. Dancers take one step forward with the right foot. Then they slide the foot back. They keep it flat on the floor. When the right foot is even with the left foot, dancers shift their weight. They pop up the left heel. Then they step forward with the left foot.

Gliding starts with a backward move. Dancers begin with the right foot flat on the floor. The left foot is on the ball of the foot. The dancer presses the heel of the left foot down. The right foot pushes backward. The dancer's weight is on the left foot. Then the dancer drags the right toe forward. When the dancer puts the heel down, the left foot glides back. Gliding looks like smoothly walking in place.

Gliding is an easy move.

BASICS OF HIP-HOP

Hip-Hop Safety

Hip-hop dancers use many muscles. People can lift weights to become strong. This helps dancers stay safe.

Balance is also important. That's because dancers might balance on their hands or heads.

Wearing the appropriate shoes and clothing can help dancers stay safe.

Dancers should not skip warming up.

Having good balance keeps people from falling and hurting themselves.

Dancers can wear protective gear. They do this when learning certain moves. For example, helmets and wrist guards protect dancers.

People need to warm up before dancing. This gets their bodies ready for exercise. People can do running or jumping exercises. Stretches are important too.

BASICS OF JAZZ

Jazz dance is performed to jazz music. This music became popular in the 1920s and 1930s. Rhythm is important in jazz music. It is also important in jazz dance. Jazz dancers can perform by themselves or in a group.

Jazz influenced other dance styles such as disco.

Jazz shoes should fit to a dancer's feet like socks.

Jazz dancers wear comfortable clothes. Their clothes should be stretchy. This lets a dancer's body move. Some jazz dancers don't wear shoes. Others wear dance sneakers or slip-on jazz shoes. Jazz shoes have soft, bendable leather. They fit snugly on the feet. They usually have a small heel.

BASICS OF JAZZ

Many jazz moves require dancers to bend their knees.

Key Movements

Jazz dancers stay close to the ground. They often keep their knees bent. Polyrhythm is important in jazz. This means two body parts move to different rhythms at the same time. Dancers can practice clapping their hands in a steady three-beat pattern. Then they tap their foot only two times over the three beats. Dancers clap and tap on beat one. Then they clap on beat two.

They tap on two and a half. Then they clap on beat three. This is polyrhythm.

Jazz dance also uses isolations. This is usually done in the beginning of the class as a warm-up. Dancers can isolate their heads, shoulders, or hips.

Advanced jazz dancers improvise. This means the dancers do not follow choreography. Instead, dancers respond to the music. They move based on the sounds they hear.

Improvising can help a dancer go outside her comfort zone.

BASICS OF JAZZ

The grapevine is a jazz step. Dancers step to the side with their right foot. Then they cross their left foot over the right foot. They step again with their right foot. The ball of the left foot touches the floor. Then they do the same steps in the opposite direction.

The jazz square is a basic step. Dancers move their feet in a square shape. Dancers step forward with their right foot. Then they cross their left foot over their right foot. They take a step to the back with the right foot. Finally, the dancer brings the left foot back. The dancer lands on the ball of the left foot. This finishes the square pattern.

Practicing daily can give dancers confidence.

Spotting

Dancers have a trick to keep from getting dizzy while turning. It is called spotting. A dancer focuses on a spot. As he turns his body, he keeps his head in the same spot. When he cannot turn any more, he whips his head around. Focusing on one spot keeps him from getting dizzy.

The pivot turn helps dancers switch directions. Dancers step forward with one foot. They place their weight on the balls of their feet. Then they turn their body to face the opposite direction. They take another step forward. Then they turn to face the original direction.

Learning with other people can help dancers grasp key movements faster.

BASICS OF JAZZ

A chassé is a move that uses two basic steps. The dance move looks like a gallop. Dancers step to the right. They bring the left foot to

In most jazz moves, dancers need to point their feet.

Dance teachers give people advice on their movements.

meet their right. They step to their right again. The left foot chases their right foot. A rock step often follows. That's when dancers use the ball of their left foot. They place it behind their right foot. The right foot can lift off the ground. Then they shift their weight forward to land on their right foot.

BASICS OF TAP

In tap, dancers tap to the beat of the music. They use their shoes to make these sounds. They usually tap their feet on a hard surface. Tap dancers can dance alone or in groups.

The bottoms of tap shoes have metal taps. The taps are on the heel and toe. The taps are held to the shoes with screws. These screws are adjustable. This lets shoes make different sounds. Loose screws make light, ringing sounds. Tight screws make deep, echoing sounds. Dancers use screwdrivers to tighten loose screws.

Tap dancers make music when they dance.

BASICS OF TAP

Show tap can be used to tell a story.

There are two forms of tap. In rhythm tap, dancers tap without music. This style focuses more on sounds than movements. Show tap is more about the way the dance looks. Facial expressions and hand movements are important. Show tap is also called Broadway tap. It is common in musical theater.

It is important for dancers to make sure their tap shoes are clean. Dancers should remove dust and floor wax from their shoes. This can be done with a damp cloth.

Most tap dancers wear T-shirts and pants to tap class. The pants should not be too long. Long pants could get caught on the taps of the shoes. This can be dangerous. Tap dancers may wear leotards. This clothing lets teachers see body movements.

Tap shoes should only be worn inside.

BASICS OF TAP

Key Movements

The two basic tap dance steps are called heel-step and step-heel. The heel-step is like walking. A dancer steps forward. The heel touches the ground first. Then the front of the foot touches the ground. The heel and the toe create different sounds. Step-heel is the opposite. The ball of the foot comes down first. Then the heel presses down.

Beginners learn how to step-heel.

The show *42nd Street* features lots of tap dancing.

BASICS OF TAP

The shuffle combines two moves called the brush and the strike. Dancers stand on one foot. They swing the other foot forward. The ball of their foot brushes the floor. Then their foot swings backward. It brushes the floor again. This is called a strike. Dancers do not use the heel. They use only the ball of the foot.

Ball change is an important move. It is when dancers shift their weight from one foot to the other. Dancers first stand on the balls of both feet. They place one foot behind and rock back onto the ball of that foot. The other foot lifts off the ground.

The buffalo is a more advanced step. It shifts weight from one foot to the other. Dancers hop

FUN FACT!

Before modern tap shoes, dancers nailed pennies into the soles of their shoes. The pennies helped make the tapping sound.

onto the right foot. Next, they do a shuffle with the left foot. Then they hop onto the left foot. The right foot crosses in front of the left foot.

Learning key movements can help dancers train for advanced moves.

ALL ABOUT BALLET

Ballet is a dance of light and airy movements. Dancers have excellent posture. Extended arms and legs make long lines. Dancers seem to float on air. "Ballet" comes from the Italian word *balletto*. It means "to dance." Ballet began

Good posture is important in ballet.

King Louis XIV was a dancer.

in the 1400s in Italy. Then it spread north to France. Louis XIV was a French king. He danced ballet. He started the first ballet school. This is why ballet terms are in French today.

ALL ABOUT BALLET

Many classical ballets, including *Don Quixote*, have detailed costumes and stage sets.

Famous Ballets

A ballet is a story told through ballet dance. Ballets are usually set to classical music. Classical music is European music from about 1750 to 1830. In a ballet, the music does not have words. The dancers' actions tell the story. A dancer who places her hands over her heart is in love. A dancer whose hands are folded is begging for mercy. A dancer who circles his hands above his head invites others to dance.

Many famous ballets were made in the 1800s. They include *Coppélia* and *Giselle*. Pyotr Ilyich Tchaikovsky was a Russian composer. He wrote the music for three ballets that are still famous today. They are *Swan Lake*, *The Nutcracker*, and *The Sleeping Beauty*.

The Nutcracker is one of the most famous ballets. It is about a young girl named Clara.

People often watch *The Nutcracker* during Christmastime.

ALL ABOUT BALLET

She gets a nutcracker as a present on Christmas Eve. At midnight, her nutcracker comes to life as a prince. The prince fights an evil mouse king. Then he takes Clara on a journey to places like the Magical Forest and the Kingdom of Sweets.

Swan Lake is the story of Princess Odette. An evil sorcerer turns her into a swan. But at night she becomes human again. A prince named Siegfried sees Odette turn from a swan into a princess. He falls in love with her. Siegfried and Odette work to break the spell.

Dancers in *Swan Lake* use their arms like wings.

In 2019, Jean-Christophe Maillot reimagined the classic *Coppélia*. Instead of Coppélia being a doll, she was a robot.

Coppélia is about a doll made by a toymaker. He loves the doll like a daughter. He wants her to come to life, but she never does. Franz is a boy in the village. He falls in love with Coppélia. But he does not know she is a doll, because she looks like a real girl.

Today, people add twists to these classic ballets. Choreographers change the dances. Sometimes they add new parts. Music composers use modern sounds. This keeps ballet fresh and exciting for today's audiences.

ALL ABOUT BALLET

Anna Pavlova

Anna Pavlova knew she wanted to dance ballet when she saw *The Sleeping Beauty*. She was a professional dancer by the 1900s. She is famous for bringing ballet to countries that had never seen it. She did this by traveling the world. Her most famous role was in a piece called *The Dying Swan*. She performed this dance about 4,000 times.

The Dying Swan was a solo performance by Anna Pavlova.

Mikhail Baryshnikov danced *The Nutcracker* in the 1970s.

Mikhail Baryshnikov

Mikhail Baryshnikov is a famous dancer known for his precise movements. He learned to dance in Russia. He toured the world. When he came to the United States, he danced at the American Ballet Theatre (ABT) and the New York City Ballet. He starred in classical ballets and in movies such as *The Turning Point* and *That's Dancing*. These helped make him even more well known.

ALL ABOUT BALLET

Misty Copeland was in the movie *The Nutcracker and the Four Realms* in 2018.

Misty Copeland

Misty Copeland is a famous ballerina. She was 13 when she started ballet. Most dancers start when they are much younger. But Copeland learned very quickly. She became a principal dancer at the ABT when she was 33. Principal dancers are the lead dancers in their ballet company. Copeland was the first Black female principal at the ABT. She is famous for dancing *Firebird*.

Marianela Núñez

Marianela Núñez is from Argentina. She started dancing lead roles when she was 14. She joined the Royal Ballet in England in 1997. In 2022, she became a principal dancer in the Royal Ballet. She has danced lead roles in *Giselle, Don Quixote*, and *The Sleeping Beauty*.

Marianela Núñez celebrated her 20 years with the Royal Ballet in 2018.

ALL ABOUT BALLET

Ballet Companies

There are ballet companies all over the world. France has the Paris Opera Ballet. It is one of the oldest ballet companies. Russia has the Bolshoi Ballet. It started in 1776. American Ballet Theatre is the most famous ballet company in North America.

Modern Dance

Modern dance is different than ballet. Modern dancers are usually barefoot. They perform movements that show feelings rather than tell stories. They use their bodies to twist into new poses. Modern dance typically does not use scenery or elaborate costumes. The focus is on the dancers.

The Paris Opera Ballet often performs at the Palais Garnier opera house.

Dancers need to prepare a routine for competitions.

Ballet Competitions

Ballet dancers can compete. Some competitions are small. Others are large. The Youth America Grand Prix (YAGP) is one competition. It is held in 25 US cities and eight international locations. Dancers ages nine through 20 can compete. The top 1,200 dancers go to New York. The winners get scholarships. Dancers may also get hired by a ballet company.

ALL ABOUT BALLROOM

Ballroom dancing used to be a type of dance for wealthy people.

Ballroom dance began long ago. It started in Europe. Dancers stayed in lines. They bowed and curtsied to one another. Partners came together and danced. Then they returned to the line. Partners barely touched each other. The dances have changed over time. Today, ballroom dance is made up of many dances. Each dance has its own history. These dances come from all over the world.

The waltz became popular in the 1800s.

ALL ABOUT BALLROOM

Hip movements are key in the cha-cha.

The slow waltz was the first dance to use the closed hold. This is when partners face each other. The lead's left hand holds the follow's right hand. The lead puts his other hand

FUN FACT!

In *Cinderella*, a mistreated girl becomes a princess. She meets the prince at a ball. Cinderella dances a waltz with the prince.

on the follow's back. The follow puts her free hand on the lead's shoulder. Couples glide and turn around the dance floor. The music is counted in groups of three beats.

Another type of waltz is the Viennese waltz. The Viennese waltz is also counted in three. But it is much faster than the slow waltz. The dancers must spin around the floor quickly. Viennese waltz is more difficult to learn than the slow waltz.

The cha-cha is a dance that began in Cuba. It used to be called the cha-cha-cha. The name comes from the triple step, which is an important move in the dance.

Salsa

Salsa is a Latin dance. Dancers move in a pattern. They take two quick steps and one slow step. They keep their upper bodies straight. They move their hips.

ALL ABOUT BALLROOM

Fred Astaire and Ginger Rogers

Fred Astaire and Ginger Rogers were famous ballroom dancers. They danced in the 1930s and 1940s. They first made a movie called *Flying Down to Rio*. Their dance scenes made them very popular. They ended up making ten movies together. One of their most well-known dances was called the foxtrot. This is a type of ballroom dance.

Fred Astaire and Ginger Rogers's onscreen chemistry made them famous.

ALL ABOUT BALLROOM

Derek and Julianne Hough

Derek and Julianne Hough are siblings. They started ballroom dancing when they were children. They danced on a TV show called *Dancing with the Stars*. Derek won on the show six times. Julianne won twice.

In 2015, Derek and Julianne Hough won Emmy awards for their choreography in *Dancing with the Stars*.

Riccardo Cocchi and Yulia Zagoruychenko started dancing together in 2007.

Riccardo Cocchi and Yulia Zagoruychenko

Riccardo Cocchi and Yulia Zagoruychenko are ten-time world champions in Latin Ballroom. Cocchi is from Italy. Zagoruychenko is from Russia. They are known for their accurate and energetic moves. The pair won their final title in in 2019.

FUN FACT!

The winners of *Dancing with the Stars* get the Mirror Ball trophy.

ALL ABOUT BALLROOM

Ballroom competitions often have 12 couples per round.

Ballroom Competitions

In ballroom competitions, dancers are put into different groups. There are age groups and skill groups. This helps dancers compete at the correct level. Advanced steps are allowed only for advanced dancers.

Dancers go onto the floor together. The music starts. Then they dance. A competition number is pinned to the lead's back. Judges watch the dancers. They look at posture and frame.

They watch for good partnering skills. They also look for proper footwork. Judges determine which dancers are the best.

There are two kinds of ballroom dance. These are American and International ballroom dance. American ballroom is usually danced in the United States and Canada. International ballroom is used throughout the world.

American ballroom has smooth and rhythm dance categories. American smooth dances have strong frame and posture. Dancers use the whole floor. These dances may be done in an open or closed hold. American smooth dances are the waltz, tango, foxtrot, and Viennese waltz. American rhythm dances focus on hip action.

FUN FACT!

The tango first became popular in Buenos Aires, Argentina. It was a common dance among European immigrants.

ALL ABOUT BALLROOM

These dances include the cha-cha, rumba, bolero, swing, and mambo.

International ballroom has standard and Latin dance categories. Standard dancers use the whole dance floor. They move at a slow pace.

Smooth dancers can break frame while standard dancers cannot.

Dancers compete in the juvenile Latin program in Belarus.

They dance the waltz, tango, foxtrot, Viennese waltz, and quickstep. Latin dancers move at a faster pace. The music is energetic. Latin dancers focus on hip action. There are five types of Latin dances. They are cha-cha, samba, rumba, jive, and paso doble.

ALL ABOUT HIP-HOP

Hip-hop started in the 1970s in the Bronx area of New York City. It was a time of change in the city. Many businesses closed. People lost their jobs. Violence was on the rise. Immigrant neighborhoods suffered the most. With businesses closed, young people had to entertain themselves. They met in empty buildings or parking lots. They played music. They laid down cardboard to break dance on.

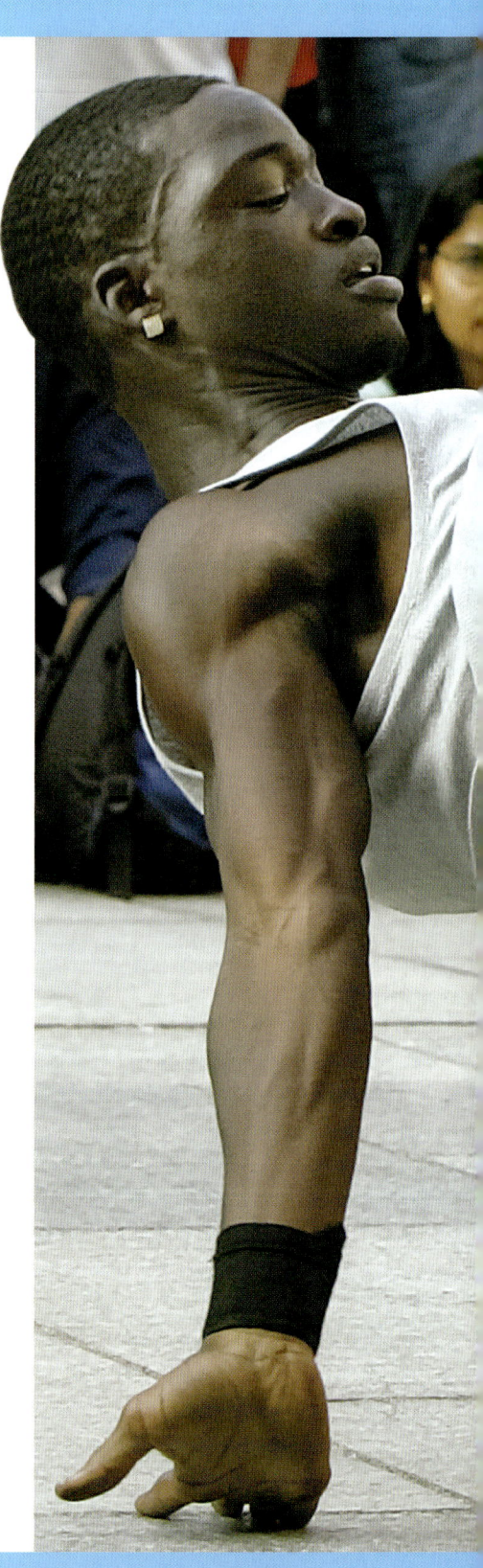

Hip-hop is performed in the streets.

ALL ABOUT HIP-HOP

The group Run-DMC influenced the culture of hip-hop.

Hip-Hop Culture

Hip-hop is more than a dance. It is a culture. There are four parts of hip-hop culture. They are DJs, graffiti, MCs, and break dancers.

K-Pop

K-pop is a kind of dance performed to K-pop music. K-pop celebrates a culture just as hip-hop does. Korean culture mixes with hip-hop, rock, and Latin music. Groups such as BTS have made K-pop popular in America.

DJ stands for disc jockey. DJs play music for dancers. Graffiti is visual art made with spray paint in public places. MC stands for master of ceremonies. The MC raps while the music plays. MCs also beatbox. Break dancers are the performers.

FUN FACT!

Beatboxing is when a person uses her voice and mouth to make rhythmic sounds.

Hip-hop is a social dance.

ALL ABOUT HIP-HOP

History of Styles

Breaking began on the streets of New York City during the 1960s and 1970s. Some of its moves came from gymnastics and martial arts. Breaking became more popular as artists like Michael Jackson used the dance steps.

Locking was invented by Don Campbell. He lived in Los Angeles, California. His friends taught him a dance called the robot shuffle. But Campbell could not remember the next step. So, he froze in place. Campbell formed

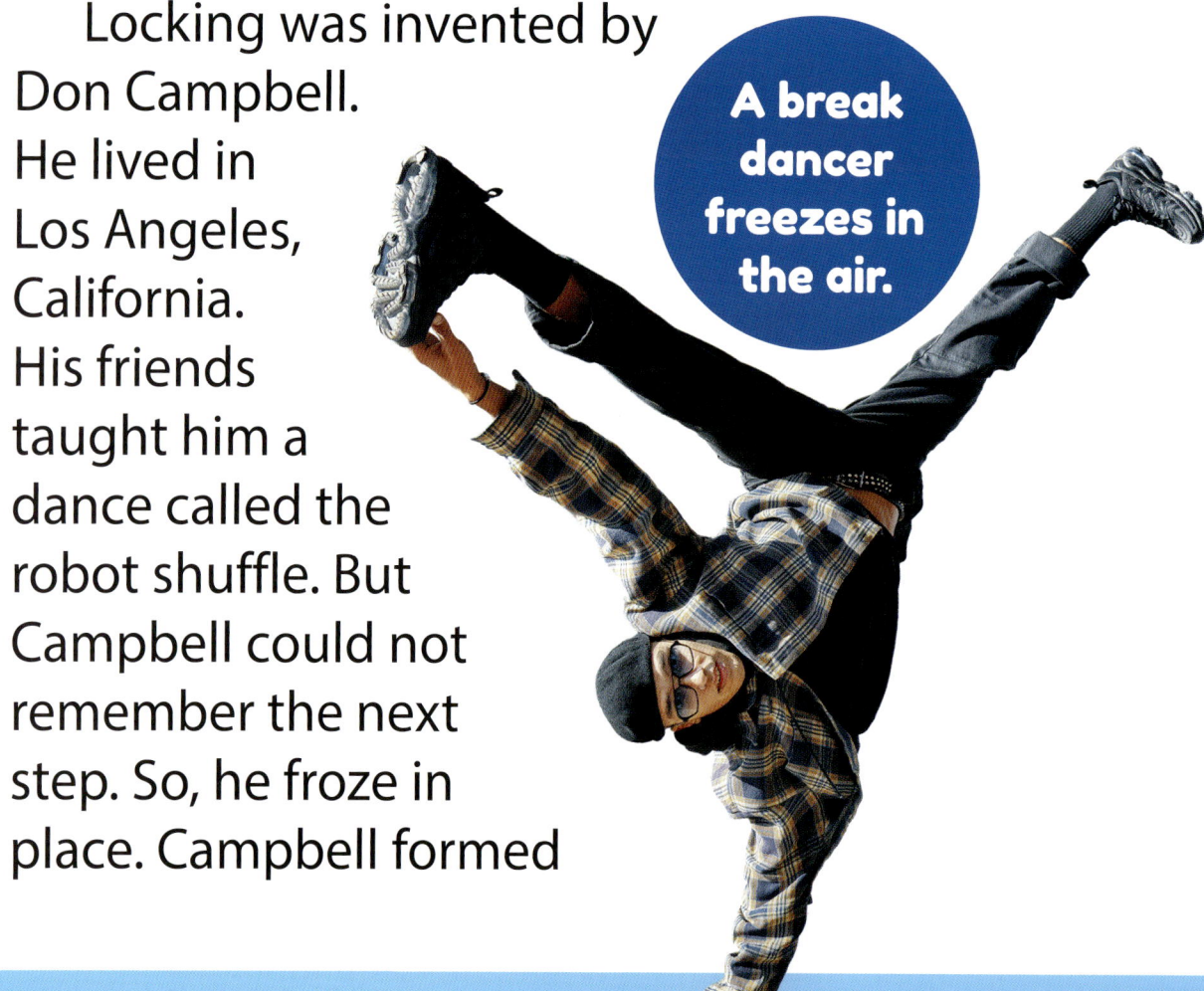

A break dancer freezes in the air.

a dance group called the Lockers. They wore striped socks and big hats. They had fancy pants and shoes. Some locking dancers wear those things today.

Popping started in California. Sam Solomon danced with a group called the Electric Boogaloos. He was called "Boogaloo Sam." He had seen locking. He wanted to create a new dance. He mixed fluid moves with isolations. Then flexed his muscles to use sharp movements. This is known as popping today. Popping is often done with locking.

The Electric Boogaloos formed in 1977.

ALL ABOUT HIP-HOP

Les Twins are brothers Larry and Laurent Bourgeois.

Les Twins

Les Twins are twin brothers from France. They were backup dancers for Beyoncé. Now they have their own act. They won a TV competition called *World of Dance* in 2017. They won $1 million. They star in music videos and movies, including *Men in Black: International*.

Clive Campbell

Clive Campbell was a break dancer. In the 1970s, he became a DJ. People called him DJ Kool Herc. He wanted to make music for break dancers. He used records and turntables. He created breaks in the music so the dancers could show their skills.

Clive Campbell came to New York City from Kingston, Jamaica.

ALL ABOUT HIP-HOP

Competitions

Hip-hop dancers compete in battles. They want to see who is the best. There are different types of competitions. For example, there is a World Locking Battle. There is also a World Popping Battle. More than 4,000 dancers compete from all over the world.

FUN FACT!

In 2020, the International Olympic Committee announced that breaking would be part of the 2024 Paris Olympics.

Many dance groups compete in the World Hip Hop Dance Championships.

ALL ABOUT JAZZ

Jazz dance became popular in the 1900s.

Jazz dance began in Africa. White European slave traders brought Africans to the Americas as slaves. Many African people lost their families, their homes, and their ways of life. Enslaved people blended their cultures together. Dance and music were important parts of their identities. They clapped their hands. They stamped their feet. These elements became part of what is known as jazz today.

Jazz music started in New Orleans, Louisiana, in the 1800s. A jazz dance craze swept New York City in the 1910s. Some musicians took jazz music and made it faster and louder. Jazz music played in musicals and movies.

Jazz dance has changed throughout time. It combined with different styles of dance. This is why there are so many kinds of jazz dance. Classical jazz is based on ballet and modern dance. It has a lot of hip and chest movements. Theatrical jazz is another kind of jazz. It is also called performance jazz dance. It is known to include elements of storytelling. Broadway shows use performance jazz.

Swing

Swing dances are partner dances to jazz music. Swing dancers can lift their partners off the ground. They may flip their partners over their heads. They flip their partners around their backs. They dip them low to the ground.

ALL ABOUT JAZZ

Jazz clubs spread across New York City's Harlem in the 1900s.

Acro

Acro dance uses jazz, ballet, and contemporary dance. It also uses gymnastics. Acro dancers add tricks such as cartwheels. They do headstands and walk on their hands. A group dance might include making a pyramid out of dancers.

Contemporary jazz mixes jazz and contemporary dance. This kind of jazz blends with classical ballet and modern dance moves. Dancers can use their bodies in many ways.

People can dance jazz in many ways.

ALL ABOUT JAZZ

Bob Fosse

Bob Fosse was a famous jazz dancer. He was also known for his choreography. Fosse choreographed for films and Broadway shows. *Chicago* and *The Pajama Game* were two of his famous musicals. *Cabaret* was a movie he choreographed. Fosse was known for dressing his dancers in hats and gloves. Fosse dancers snapped their fingers. They used turned-in knees and toes. They used shoulder rolls. Fosse-style choreography is still famous today.

Bob Fosse was a famous director and choreographer.

Katherine Dunham choreographed for Broadway, opera, and film.

Katherine Dunham

Katherine Dunham taught jazz dancers. She used African, South American, and Caribbean moves.

ALL ABOUT JAZZ

Dunham started her own dance method. It was called the Dunham technique. This combined classical ballet with Caribbean and African styles of dance.

Dunham was the lead dancer in her own dance company. Dancers in her company went on Broadway. They also danced in movies, such as *Cabin in the Sky* and *Stormy Weather*.

Alvin Ailey

Alvin Ailey was one of Dunham's students. He became a famous dancer and choreographer. His dances often had big jumps and dramatic hand movements. He started a dance company in 1958 called the Alvin Ailey American Dance Theater.

Ailey's work often told stories of his own life and African American culture. One of his most well-known works is called *Revelations*. The dance piece includes Black spiritual and blues.

Alvin Ailey, *right*, strikes a pose with actor John Travolta.

ALL ABOUT JAZZ

Jazz Competitions

The Jazz Dance World Congress meets for five days. People who love jazz dance come together. Teachers work with jazz students. Professional dancers perform. They come from all over the world.

Starpower International Talent and Dance Competition looks for talent. It has competitions in three levels. Dancers compete in different dance styles. Jazz is one of the styles.

Competitions show lots of unique costumes.

ALL ABOUT TAP

Tap dance has roots in many dance styles, including flamenco.

Tap dance came from the United States. But it has roots in many different cultures. Clogging is a dance from England, Ireland, and Scotland. Clog dancers wear shoes with wooden heels. Dancers keep rhythm with the heels of their shoes. Flamenco is a dance from Spain. Clapping, foot stomping, and hand movements are important in flamenco. West

Flamenco

Flamenco is a stomping dance from Spain. Dancers stomp their feet in hard-soled shoes. Hand clapping is also important. Dancers slap their palms for loud claps. They cup their hands for soft claps.

African step dances use flowing body movement. They use tapping footsteps. Tap is influenced by all of these styles.

Tap dance became popular with the golden age of musicals. This was during the 1930s and 1940s. Actors sang and tap-danced onstage. In the 1950s, tap lost its popularity. But by the 1960s, people became interested in tap again. Some TV shows featured programs that showed tap.

Tap dance changed as people watched and copied other tap dancers. They sometimes took the old steps and changed them into something new. This continues today. Although there are key tap movements, dancers are able to add on and change these steps.

FUN FACT!

The Rockettes are a dance company in New York City. They are known for their kick line dance. But all Rockettes must know how to dance ballet, jazz, and tap.

ALL ABOUT TAP

Bill Robinson

Bill "Mr. Bojangles" Robinson was a vaudeville actor in the early 1900s. Vaudeville actors could sing, dance, and do comedy. In the 1920s, Robinson went to Broadway. He starred in *Blackbirds of 1928*. In 1935, he was in a movie called *The Little Colonel*. He performed a tap dance on a flight of stairs. It became famous. National Tap Dance Day is celebrated every year on his birthday, May 25.

> Bill Robinson was one of the most famous tap dancers in the early 1900s.

Gene Kelly, *right*, and Debbie Reynolds, *left*, starred in *Singin' in the Rain* together.

Gene Kelly

Gene Kelly was a famous tap dancer in the 1930s through the early 1950s. His tap dancing was based on clogging and the Irish jig. He choreographed tap dances. He tap danced on Broadway in shows like *One for the Money* and *The Time of Your Life*. He starred in films like *Singin' in the Rain*.

ALL ABOUT TAP

Gregory Hines was a tap dancer, singer, and actor.

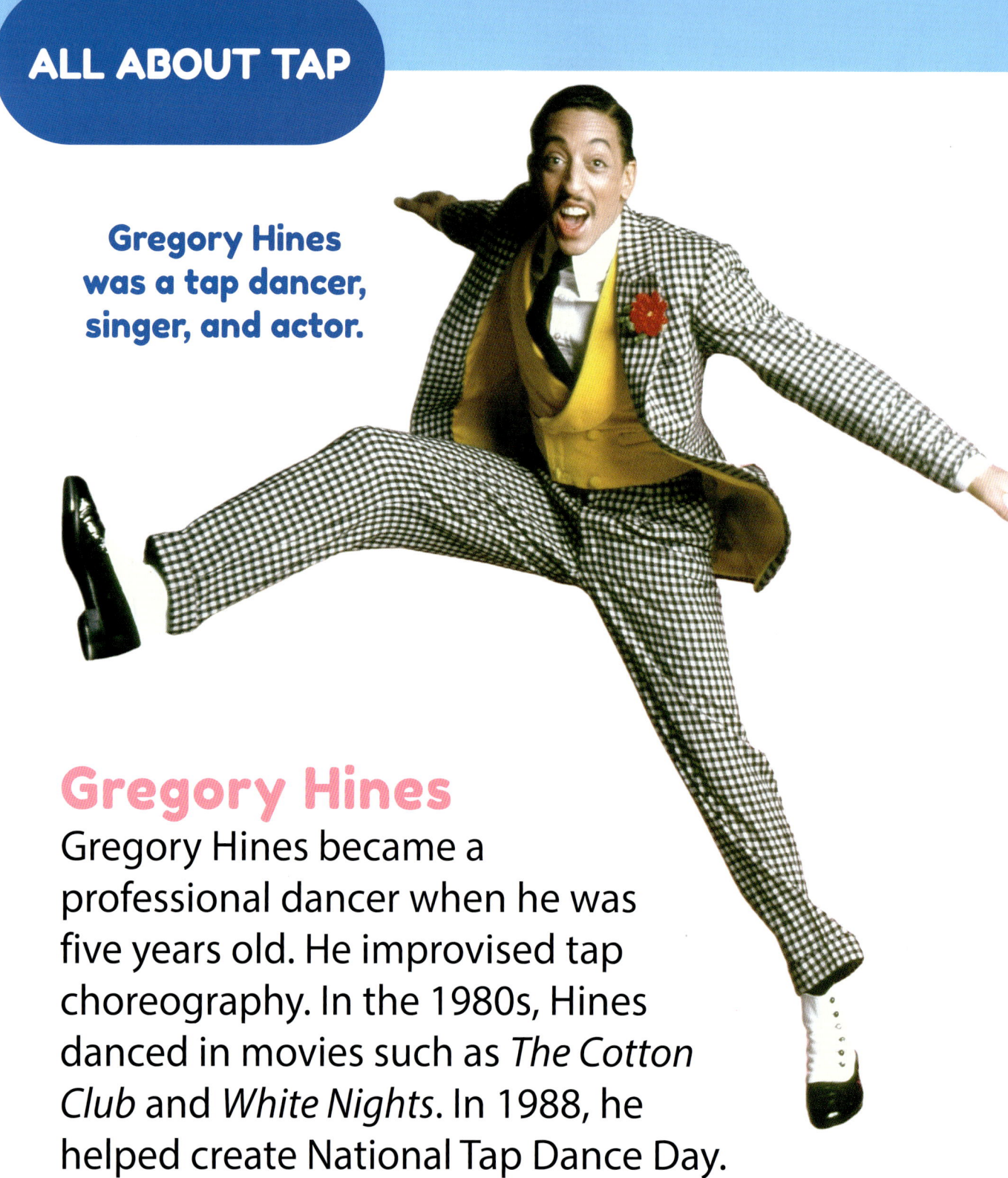

Gregory Hines

Gregory Hines became a professional dancer when he was five years old. He improvised tap choreography. In the 1980s, Hines danced in movies such as *The Cotton Club* and *White Nights*. In 1988, he helped create National Tap Dance Day.

Savion Glover

Savion Glover started dancing on Broadway at nine years old. He does not just use his heels and toes. He also uses the arches and the balls of his feet. Glover works in movies too. He helped think of tap dance moves for the penguins in the 2006 movie *Happy Feet*. Glover also teaches his own tap classes.

Savion Glover is a well-known dancer and choreographer.

ALL ABOUT TAP

Competitions

A tap dancer is called a hoofer. Hoofers compete in challenges. One dancer taps. Another hoofer watches and listens. Then he or she tries to copy the dance. The person also tries make the dance even better. Tap dancers also compete in formal competitions. Companies such as Starpower or Legacy hold dance competitions around the country. Tap is a dance category at these competitions.

Irish Dance

Irish dance began in Ireland. Dancers wear dresses, kilts, or pants with jackets. Hard shoes called hornpipe shoes make a tapping sound. A show called *Riverdance* helped Irish dance gain global fame.

Dancers need to make sure their tap shoes fit.

Tap dancers compete in the Joinville Dance Festival, a big dance competition in Brazil.

ALL ABOUT DANCING FOR LIFE

Some people want to dance professionally. This means they get paid to dance. Dancers get jobs dancing in musicals. They may be in music videos or TV commercials.

Some dancers are hired by dance companies. These usually focus on one kind of dance. The companies may stay in one city or travel from place to place. Many dance students dream of becoming famous. But very few succeed at this level.

People can dance in their free time.

There are other ways to have a job in dance. Some dancers choose to study dance in college and earn a degree. Then they can get hired as dance teachers. Others become choreographers. They create dances for others to perform. Teachers and choreographers are important. They help keep the art of dance alive.

Anyone can dance.

ALL ABOUT DANCING FOR LIFE

People of all ages go to dance classes.

Dance does not need to be a job. It can be a hobby. People of all ages can take dance classes for fun. Dancers can use their skills in community theaters.

Other people like to go to social dances. These are held in large spaces. Some have live music. People practice what they learned in class. They meet and dance with new people. Anyone can have fun by dancing.

IF You like telling stories through dance, **THEN** Try ballet.

IF You like making up moves, **THEN** Try jazz or hip-hop.

IF You like drumming, **THEN** Try tap.

IF You like full body movement, **THEN** Try hip-hop or tap.

IF You like to stand tall, **THEN** Try ballet or ballroom.

IF You like dancing with a partner, **THEN** Try ballroom.

GLOSSARY

battle
A competition between two break dancers.

Broadway
The name of a street in New York City where many theaters are located.

choreography
The planned steps of a dance.

competition
A contest in which dancers are judged to see who is the best.

composer
A person who creates music.

contemporary
Happening in the present time.

immigrant
A person who comes to live in a different country.

improvise
To work on a dance without planned steps.

musical
A play or movie in which singing and dancing are essential.

posture
How to hold the body while standing or sitting.

sole
The bottom part of a person's foot.

technique
Movement with skill and purpose.

TO LEARN MORE

More Books to Read

Murray, Julie. *Competitive Dance*. Abdo, 2023.

Robbins, Dean. *¡Mambo Mucho Mambo! The Dance That Crossed Color Lines*. Candlewick, 2021.

Vanden Branden, Claire. *Dance*. Abdo, 2020.

Online Resources

To learn more about dance, please visit **abdobooklinks.com** or scan this QR code. These links are routinely monitored and updated to provide the most current information available.

INDEX

ballet, 12, 14, 18–25, 70–81, 105, 107, 110, 115, 125

ballroom, 26–41, 82–93, 125

Broadway, 64, 105, 108, 110, 116–117, 119

choreography, 7, 32, 57, 75, 108, 110, 117–118, 123

hip-hop, 14, 42–53, 94–102, 125

jazz, 14, 54–61, 104–112, 115, 125

tap, 62–69, 114–120, 125

PHOTO CREDITS

Cover Photos: Shutterstock Images, front (left); Kevin Winter/Getty Images for The Recording Academy/Getty Images Entertainment/Getty Images, front (center); Maria Moroz/Shutterstock Images, front (right); Rachata Teyparsit/Shutterstock Images, front (background); Perfect Angle Images/Shutterstock Images, back

Interior Photos: iStockphoto, 1, 9, 12, 13, 24, 27, 34, 41, 45, 97, 120, 122, 123, 125 (bottom); Shutterstock Images, 3, 4, 8, 11 (bottom left), 14, 16, 17, 21, 25, 26, 29, 30, 31, 32, 37, 40, 43 (top left), 43 (top right), 43 (bottom left), 43 (bottom right), 48, 51, 58, 80, 84, 90, 114, 124; A. Lesik/Shutterstock Images, 5, 74; GAS Photo/Shutterstock Images, 6; Shaikh Meraj/Shutterstock Images, 7; Jack F./iStockphoto, 10, 38; Connie T Ballash/iStockphoto, 11 (top); Richard Semik/Shutterstock Images, 11 (bottom right); VG Stock Studio/Shutterstock Images, 18; Kim Kelley-Wagner/Shutterstock Images, 19; Light Wave Media/Shutterstock Images, 22 (left), 22 (right), 23 (left), 23 (middle), 23 (right); Mihail Siergiejevicz/Shutterstock Images, 28; Dmitry Morgan/Shutterstock Images, 33, 93; Red Line Editorial, 35; Africa Studio/Shutterstock Images, 36; Oleg Shakirov/Shutterstock Images, 39; Aaron Amat/iStockphoto, 42; Gino Santa Maria/Shutterstock Images, 44; Tom Merton/iStockphoto, 46 (top), 125 (middle right); Roman Chazov/Shutterstock Images, 46 (bottom); Jeff Pachoud/AFP/Getty Images, 47; Leika Production/Shutterstock Images, 49; Pavel L Photo and Video/Shutterstock Images, 50, 69; Adam Kaz/iStockphoto, 52, 56, 59, 61, 65; Yagi Studio/iStockphoto, 53; Sean Nel/Shutterstock Images, 54, 60, 125 (top left); KBYC Photography/Shutterstock Images, 55; Pavel Rumme/Shutterstock Images, 57; Wave Break Media/Shutterstock Images, 62; Alen Kadr/Shutterstock Images, 63; Timothy A. Clary/AFP/Getty Images, 64; Claire McAdams/Shutterstock Images, 66; Steve Parsons/WPA Pool/Getty Images Entertainment/Getty Images, 67; Drazen Zigic/Shutterstock Images, 70; Everett Collection/Shutterstock Images, 71; Vince Caligiuri/Getty Images Entertainment/Getty Images, 72; Yasuyoshi Chiba/AFP/Getty Images, 73; Samuel de Roman/Getty Images Entertainment/Getty Images, 75; Bettmann/Getty Images, 76, 77, 82, 86–87, 104, 106, 109, 116; Matt Winkelmeyer/Getty Images Entertainment/Getty Images, 78; John Phillips/Getty Images for The Royal Ballet/Getty Images Entertainment/Getty Images, 79; Mohd Rasfan/AFP/Getty Images, 81; Photo Josse/Leemage/Corbis Historical/Getty Images, 83; Chris Pizzello/Invision/AP Images, 88; Nigel Roddis/Getty Images News/Getty Images, 89; Vladimir Vasiltvich/Shutterstock Images, 92; Michael Dwyer/AP Images, 94–95; Dave Hogan/Hulton Archive/Getty Images, 96; Viktor Gladkov/iStockphoto, 98; i4images_music/Alamy, 99; Dean Treml/Red Bull via Getty Images/Handout/Getty Images Entertainment/Getty Images, 100; Steven Ferdman/Getty Images Entertainment/Getty Images, 101; Isaac Brekken/AP Images, 102–103; Lorraine Swanson/Shutterstock Images, 107, 125 (top right); John Springer Collection/Corbis Historical/Getty Images, 108; AP Images, 111; Fausto Marci/Alamy, 112; Hero Images Inc./Alamy, 113; Silver Screen Collection/Hulton Archive/Moviepix/Getty Images, 117; Jack Mitchell/Archive Photos/Getty Images, 118; Neilson Barnard/Getty Images for the 2015 Tribeca Film Festival/Getty Images Entertainment/Getty Images, 119; Mister Shadow/Agencia Estado/AP Images, 121; Michelle D. Milliman/Shutterstock Images, 125 (middle left)